EDGE
of the
ABYSS

The Usefulness of Antichrist Terminology
in the Era of Donald Trump

Robert Isaac Skidmore, Ph.D., M.Div.

CHIRON PUBLICATIONS • ASHEVILLE, NORTH CAROLINA

www.ChironPublications.com

Interior and cover design by Danijela Mijailovic
Printed primarily in the United States of America.

ISBN 978-1-63051-895-0 paperback
ISBN 978-1-63051-896-7 hardcover
ISBN 978-1-63051-897-4 electronic
ISBN 978-1-63051-898-1 limited edition paperback

Library of Congress Cataloging-in-Publication Data Pending

Table of Contents

Foreword

*Never can true reconcilement grow where
wounds of deadly hate have pierced so deep . . .*

John Milton, *Paradise Lost*

Currently in our society, we are the witnesses of tumultuous times full of contemptuous behavior—some of which we are drawn into. In our journalistic "post-fairness doctrine" era, world and national events play out over largely partisan airwaves, sometimes to the point people cannot tell (or barely can tell) whether they are even discussing the same developments. Further, the instantaneous reaction that includes one's complete rightness and the "other's" utter depravity and wrongness is an

1

everyday event. Social media seem to lend themselves to an increased brashness toward others not seen when we are in one another's presence. These increasingly polarizing stances are frequently observed with hypersensitive defensiveness, which plays into devaluing an important role of the press—its commitment to question and criticize authority. This important function of the press—to ensure that we are not manipulated and controlled—has been devalued and dismissed in a manner characterized by such automatized responses as the now familiar phrase "fake news" when the press questions those we are affiliated with politically. News is now consumed as to whether it offers some elusive form of objective "truth," almost as if the standards of truth the news presents must fit one's beliefs, rather than function to critically question and analyze political leaders.

At the same time, other news outlets knowingly play into the extreme partisanship and profit from propagandistic, slanderous, and yellow journalistic views that their consumers "want" to hear. Subscribers rarely listen to the "other side" and reinforce their biases by only listening to or reading a continuous flow of "news" that rarely challenges them beyond those very biases. This becomes a dangerously ominous sign in a nation when increasingly large groups in conflict rely heavily on a particularly partisan political identification or ideology to inform their thinking. Behind the obvious knee-jerk reactions which can, among other things, tear relationships apart, lurks a largely unreflective mind that is largely unable to be self-reflective or self-critical. Further, these kinds of stances make individuals and groups potentially quite vulnerable to being manipulated on both smaller and grander scales.

People who are unable to effectively criticize their political affiliations or evaluate whether what they are being told has any limitations, and who fear the agenda of their political opponents, often push forward, unthinkingly, into unknown territory. During times of crises or great problems, the need for leadership becomes increasingly paramount. The confluence of these forces, when combined with grasps for partisan power increases the potential for manipulation. Additionally, the need for solutions for complex and sometimes overwhelming problems can provide the conditions for seemingly simple solutions that appeal to the core of "believers" and provide relief and, at the same time, can assure that the power that is craved will be further secured.

Somewhat separate from the inner world of politics, but a critical voice of our political institutions, is an outside force whose understandable cynicism about the failures of these very same politics gives rise to a seemingly endless tide of "conspiracy theories." Those who propagate these "theories" utilize savvy methods, including technological and computer skills, to arrange a series of disconnected facts and infer all kinds of seemingly convincing ideas that have no real empirical basis, to alternatively explain current events. Many who lack critical thinking skills may be manipulated by materials that are called a theory—a name that is intended to be a description for an emerging interpretation arriving from a body of evidence that is based on empirically derived facts, not loosely applied inferences or made-up ideas. These highly influential producers can sway significant numbers of people who fall prey to their convincing—but uncritically evaluated—suggestions, such as the Earth being flat. Like partisanship, uncritical evaluations of these so-called theories make persons vulnerable to all kinds of falsehoods or partial truths that are not productive, and can be harmful and destructive.

In an age where our society becomes increasingly less curious, less analytical, and unreflective, we run the risk of giving up our right to think for ourselves and, in a sense, risk "losing our minds." In this way, losing one's mind means not thinking for oneself and therefore missing the possibility to consider the consequences of decisions made when uncritically backing the stance of political fancies. One's mind is given away or absorbed by a movement for the use of advancing other agendas of power. During times of crisis, economic duress, threats of war, and other important events, significant decisions about the future of a nation and its governance are made with little or any consideration of the consequences. This dynamic can make a whole political group, and at times an entire nation, vulnerable to high levels of manipulation. For example, in desperate times, Germany, an intelligent nation whose suffering economy and other "ills" pushed them into desperation, felt it needed swift answers to save them from their troubling state. A significant number of Germans, who were looking for a redeemer and a savior, were able to be manipulated by a leader who seemed to have answers but who led the country into untold atrocities and its eventual ruin.

Our writer is positioned uniquely as one influenced by two different ontologies—the Eastern Orthodox Church and depth psychology. In this important work, the Reverend Dr. Skidmore goes a long way to help us examine many especially important levels of our current epoch. Although, based on the title of the work, one might think that the aim is to diagnose the president of the United States as the antichrist, our writer provides us with a more important analysis. By examining many of the scriptural, archetypal, political, psychopatholo-gical, group dynamics, and various other perspectives that are associated with the spirit of an age of an antichrist, he does not proclaim the president to be "the Antichrist" but demonstrably points to these very qualities that embody "the themes and functions scripturally, socially, and psychologically associated with antichrist," concluding that the president fits this description aptly.

However, this does not appear to be the major thrust of this writing. We are asked to probe yet even more deeply into the various dynamics of collective thinking and motivations. The author looks at religious, psychological, and several other dimensions that are important for each person, such as movement, ideology, and religious affiliation, to examine the greater view of the intricacies of these dynamics for a society and thus argues that we *must become aware of the spirit of our age*. To say this work points only at an individual would be to miss the point. Without understanding the collective conditions and spirit of this movement, there is no real perception of the antichrist. The masses by their very spirit, also create the antichrist. And the antichrist offers its messianic message to this collective movement, which further forms and informs the movement. Our author gifts us in this exploration of how this mutually reciprocal and reinforcing dynamic functions.

A central tenet under Skidmore's consideration is his analysis of human nature and the shadow as conceptualized by Carl Jung. Jung saw Christ as both a symbol for the *Self* but also a symbol of light, which for Jung, necessitates its dark side, a shadow of the light—antichrist. Although Jung's idea of the shadow is not necessarily evil, the shadow has the potential to become evil, as described by many depth psychologists. Evil in this context is likened to the problem of Dr. Jekyll and Mr. Hyde. As such, evil, on the Mr. Hyde side, results from being identified rather completely with the shadow. For Dr. Jekyll, evil occurs when that shadow side is completely split off from consciousness and lives on autonomously. While most individuals in our time would not think of themselves in this manner, our culture may be more caught up in the spirit of this dynamic than we realize. Collectively and individually, cultures highly polarized into categories of "Us" and "Them" accelerate the problem of shadow, which results in finding evil entirely outside of oneself. In these conditions, people may be more identified with their shadow than they are aware. Generally, this problem is solidified by a lack of conscious awareness along with a related problem, massive levels of projection of the evil that is denied onto the other.

In an apparent intersection between Holy Scripture and postmodern depth psychology, the unconscious can be inferred from Christ's words about humans who demonstrate projection, "How can you say to your brother, 'Let me remove the speck from your eye'; and look, a plank is in your own eye?" (*New King James Version*, Mat. 7:4) And, from Christ's parable, the Pharisee prays, "God, I thank You that I am not like other men—extortioners, unjust, adulterers, or even as this tax collector." (Lu. 18:11) For our age, our author would seem to strongly suggest that in any age of the spirit of the antichrist, self-examination is required and necessary, and we must remind ourselves that Christ states he did not come to call the (self-proclaimed) righteous, but sinners, to repentance. But awareness of oneself as sinner or even mistaken is impossible as long as the opposites are kept entirely apart and lack integration, as the Reverend Dr. Skidmore describes. Jung's psychology stresses the importance of unifying the opposites. Jung sees Christ as a uniter of the opposites. Jung strongly suggests that the spirit of Christ is a corrective principle, balancing the shadow—shining light into darkness, if you will (Jn. 1:4). Our author emphasizes that potentially dangerous problems with the shadow collectively or individually result when the opposites are kept entirely apart.

Thus, the value of Skidmore's work would appear to extend far beyond his diagnosis. In my view, regardless of whether the reader agrees with his conclusion, or even if our reader is a supporter of the current president, our author powerfully invites us to consider evaluating not only his rich exploration into the dynamics of the spirit of the antichrist but also the role we might play within those dynamics. I would argue that such an analysis is promising, as it offers to us a return to critical thinking that requires one to transcend political differences and move into the heart of the matter—which should go a long way toward making us less vulnerable to political influence and toward a return to having the "mind of Christ."

Steven-John M. Harris, Ph.D.
Psychologist, Private Practice
Newport Beach, CA

Introduction

I write this not because I want to but because it seems I have to. No matter how many times I cast the idea of this piece of writing aside, it returns to me as a topic that wants me to address it. The issue concerns the notion of *antichrist*, whether it is useful for us at this point in history and whether it is in any way an appropriate term for understanding and describing phenomena in the public and political realm—and, in particular, whether it is any way appropriate to use this term in describing Donald Trump.

I am a practicing Christian (or, rather, an aspiring one, because I believe Christian discipleship is a work always in progress) and, in fact, am a clergy person in the Orthodox Church—a parish priest, now, for two decades. I am also a licensed therapist, whose orientation for practice is depth psychological. I, like some others who also profess

Christianity, have been baffled by the appeal Donald Trump has for many people of faith. From the time of his candidacy in 2015 until the present, I have expressed my concerns on social media, believing until recently that his incompetence, malevolence, and deceptiveness were self-evident to any sincere observer and that reasoned argument would persuade those who, through insufficient consideration of facts, supported him or remained on the fence. I have watched with horror as he has successively traversed thresholds that, at nearly any other time in U.S. history, would have represented irreparable public scandal and political defeat.

I have eventually come to believe that Trump's appeal can only be described as something *spiritual*. By that, I mean that his influence over attitudes, behaviors, and events calls for explanations that go beyond our customary frames of reference. Regular social, political, or psychological perspectives do not seem to go far enough. Trump's successes bewilder us precisely because they occur contrary to the expectations of conventional analysis. The existence of analogous periods in history does not argue for the normalcy of what we are living through now, because those analogous periods (and, though I find comparisons to Hitler deservedly suspect, I would argue they are not groundless) fill us with the same astonishment and call, also, for a language that transcends what we normally use to describe social, psychological, and political phenomena. For particular aspects of what we currently witness, perhaps religious language is indispensable. To this end, I have for the moment put aside attempts to persuade in any way that might immediately compel and instead have focused my attention on the spiritual construct—which, in psychology, most closely parallels the notion of the *archetype*—of antichrist.

We live in an ironic period of time. Christians who for decades speculated about the possible identity of antichrist, now seem mute on the topic, right at a point when Christianity could especially benefit from the critical self-reflection the idea of antichrist perfectly engenders. Christians' neglect to honestly consider what their own tradition says about antichrist corresponds with a neglect of self-scrutiny concerning their loyalty and devotion to the current U.S. president. I will argue that the concept of antichrist, understood in scriptural, psychological, social, and archetypal contexts, retains value for contemporary religious and societal thought.

What follows is not exhaustive. The discussion of the construct of antichrist that I present is occasioned by our current societal unrest but not limited to it. The alarm I attempt to sound is intended not so much to mount an opposition to Trump's growing influence (which seems to be a foregone conclusion) as it is to stimulate consideration of the social, psychological, and spiritual dynamics I believe he embodies—which, because they express archetypal patterns, are destined to reappear in other times, places, and ways. Antichrist, as an archetypal pattern, will remain with us for a long time, surpassing the period in which Donald Trump gives us occasion to consider it. I look at this pattern from numerous angles as a kind of initial survey for those who may want to explore particular angles more closely or propose angles I don't touch upon here.

It may even happen—though I think it not likely—that a reader will disagree with my negative judgment of Trump, yet still find my reflections on antichrist of value. If this happens, I will at least console myself with the thought that my reflections have succeeded as more than just an indulgence and amplification of my own political perspective—and that, if I had made my reasoning inseparable from my conclusion, I would have also impinged upon the freedom by which a reader might arrive, possibly, at my same conclusion. This approach leaves me the power of persuasion but takes from me the power of compulsion.

I.

ANTICHRIST IN ITS THEOLOGICAL SETTING

I.

Antichrist in Its Theological Setting

Scriptural Context

Biblically speaking, the term antichrist has a more complex meaning than what popular culture often assigns to it, where it usually refers to one individual who appears at the end of days, inaugurating, heralding, and executing Satan's last surge of activity before Christ and his heavenly army appear, confronting Antichrist (capitalized, to indicate it as a personal name) and his followers in the battle of Armageddon. All of this culminates in the final divine judgment, in which God casts Satan, Antichrist, and those under Antichrist's sway into the fiery abyss. Though dozens of scriptural references refer to the same concept using other terms, the actual word *antichrist* appears only five times in Scripture (1 Jn. 2:18, 22; 4:3; 2 Jn. 2:18). All of these appearances refer to antichrist as a spirit capable of manifesting through a variety of individuals, not merely one. Passages such as 2 Thessalonians 2:2-3 convey the idea of antichrist as a single individual, "that man of sin . . . the son of perdition" (*King James Version*) who will appear before the "day of Christ"—and the book of Revelation, in numerous places, utilizes the imagery of "the beast," who speaks with the authority of "the dragon," (13:11) who corresponds with Satan. Even here, though, the "beast," commonly understood to be the antichrist—the one who marks his followers with the number 666—acts with the authority of the one referred to as "the first beast," (13:12) indicating, again, that the spirit of antichrist resides in more than just a single individual. The descriptions and imagery used to describe antichrist in the book of Revelation rely, in turn, upon imagery earlier presented in the Old Testament book of Daniel.

A chief trait of antichrist, whether it appears in a single person or multiple individuals, is its power of deception: It performs "great wonders" and "miracles" through which it "deceiveth them that dwell on the earth." (Rev. 13:13-14) 2 Thessalonians, referring to the uncanny efficacy of this deception, goes as far to suggest that God Himself enhances it, saying that He "shall send them strong delusion, that they should believe a lie." (2:11) Another distinctive feature of antichrist is its intention and ability to subvert values, blaspheming what is universally known as holy and good, and usurping the place uniquely reserved for God. He "opposeth and exalteth himself above all that is called God." (2:4)

Antichrist as Idol

The prefix in the word antichrist is *anti*, which in English commonly means "against." It can also mean, though, "instead of." This rendering opens awareness of another aspect of antichrist: He does not necessarily appear as something anti-thetical to Christ or Christianity but rather subverts the worship of Christ by effectively taking Christ's place in the hearts of those who believe themselves to be his followers. A variety of places in the New Testament bear this meaning out. Christ's words in Matthew 7:21-23 indicate the possibility of people failing to worship him, not because they follow a path that represents his opposite but because they apply his name, wrongly, to something that is in fact not him:

> Not every one that saith unto me, Lord, Lord, shall enter into the kingdom of heaven; but he that doeth the will of my Father which is in heaven. Many will say to me in that day, Lord, Lord, have we not prophesied in thy name? and in thy name have cast out devils? and in thy name done many wonderful works? And then will I profess unto them, I never knew you: depart from me, ye that work iniquity.

This theme appears in other places as well, including Matthew 24:23-27, which emphasizes "false Christs" who will appear and be mistaken, by some, for the real thing, and in Luke 13:25-30, where the day of judgment shows some as deceived about the nature of their own hearts, believing themselves, wrongly, to be Christ's disciples.

The concept of antichrist is, in this way, akin to the concept of idolatry. In particular, it evokes remembrance of how Israel, in 1 Samuel 8, insisted that God give them a king and, in the process, rejected the kingship of YHWH himself. This theme appears again in a story recounted in all four gospels (Mt. 27:15-23; Mk. 15:6-15; Lu. 23:13-20; and Jn. 18:38-40), in which Israel pleads with Pontius Pilate to release Barabbas, rather than Christ, from prison—thus consigning Christ to crucifixion.

Antichrist as Marker Between Truth and Error

It is significant that antichrist appears at the end of days, at "the last time." (1 Jn. 2:18) Its appearance indicates the utmost point in the testing of faith, in which truth itself is in peril of such effective distortion that even the faithful should lose hold of it. "Except that the Lord had shortened those days, no flesh should be saved," (Mk. 13:20) Jesus says, and he also tells us that "false Christs and false prophets shall rise, and shall shew signs and wonders, to seduce, if it *were* possible, even the elect." (Mk. 13:22) "Take ye heed, watch and pray," (v. 33) he says. He also says, "Watch ye therefore" (v. 35) and again, "watch," (v. 37) thus emphasizing how the period of the antichrist will represent the utmost testing of even Christ's most faithful followers. St. Paul, after describing antichrist's power of deception, admonishes his readers to "stand fast, and hold the traditions which ye have been taught" (2 Thess. 2:15)—indicating that the tests they will be subjected to relate to their ability to discern the truth.

With this theological context in place, we can note how the concept of antichrist functions on the boundary between truth and error, and how it particularly functions to warn us that some things on the side of error convincingly retain characteristics we associate with truth—so much so that, without deliberate effort, our normal instincts concerning truth can be confounded. Scripture's reference to antichrist serves as a warning that, not only must we guard against error, but we must ceaselessly scrutinize our perceptions of truth and error themselves. The power of deception, particularly as it reaches the extreme point represented by antichrist, is that it passes tests that, during normal times, sufficiently distinguish truth from error.

Error, in the form of antichrist, does not reveal itself except to those who are on guard, not just for error, but for trickery, for cunning and sophisticated camouflage. Those who walk on the road of antichrist may take comfort in the fact that signs saying "Truth" line this road, and those signs are indistinguishable from signs that, during usual times, accurately indicate where truth can be found. Their mistake lies in their failure to recognize that not all times are usual and that extreme situations exist in which those signs can be deliberately and maliciously manipulated. There are times when appeal to external signs cannot sufficiently determine whether one follows truth or error. The warning about antichrist is similar in kind to warnings parents may give children that danger does not appear always in the form of a scary-looking stranger, but it sometimes appears in the form of someone you know and whom you might assume you can trust. It represents the most extreme scenario in the realm of error posing as truth.

The existence of antichrist, as a concept, calls for utmost vigilance of heart and spirit. It functions as an unqualified imperative to watch and attend. Even when you appear to yourself to be doing everything well, and when you have checked off all the boxes on your tests for truth—even then, in fact, especially then, you need to remain alert, because your assurance might indicate only that the deception has infiltrated even your own powers of discernment. The warning of antichrist's presence in the world is related to the New Testament's summons to circumspection. With regard to the world, we must watch not just for wolves, but for wolves that look like sheep. "Beware of false prophets, which come to you in sheep's clothing, but inwardly they are ravening wolves." (Mt. 7:15) With regard to our internal state, we are to be suspicious even of our own faith, understanding our own hearts can deceive us. "Examine yourselves, whether ye be in the faith; prove your own selves." (2 Cor. 13:5a)

II.

ANTICHRIST
IN PUBLIC VIEW

II.

Antichrist in Public View

Sociopathy: The Psychological Correlate to Antichrist

In psychology, the *sociopath* most closely relates to the idea of antichrist—a person who consistently lacks empathy and demonstrates callousness toward the feelings of others. In individuals we describe as sociopathic, we genuinely wonder whether they have capacity for concern, so that it might emerge or be rediscovered, or if it is entirely absent. The void of empathy sometimes pairs with charm and charisma. Sociopaths often catch us off guard, and we feel momentarily stunned by the sight of someone utterly devoid of shame or humility. Perhaps evolution has not equipped us to readily recognize and respond to sociopaths because they are so rare. The *Diagnostic and Statistical Manual of Mental Disorders* (2013) of the American Psychological Association estimates they make up between 0.2% and 3.3% of the population. We often afford sociopaths the benefit of the doubt, dismissing indications of something amiss in their behavior, concluding we are mistaken in our perceptions—which makes sense in the other 99% of situations.

As a statistical outlier, the sociopath may not be detected by our customary state of caution and awareness. We may have a harder time spotting a sociopath than we do spotting a person who merely has low moral character. People of low moral character capture our attention because, despite their failure, we continue to evaluate them along the spectrum of expected behavior. However much they fail, we still categorize them as people for whom morality has relevance. We imagine there exists, perhaps deep within them, a conscience that chides them and encourages them to assume a more positive relationship to society. The sociopath may actually appear exemplary by societal standards, yet he or she operates from a different rationale than the one we usually consider when we evaluate behavior. A sociopath behaves not merely to reach familiar measures of success but to succeed at someone else's expense. For a sociopath, living up to society's values does not arise from a positive estimation of those values but from the intention to disarm people who rely on those values for their assessment of character in those they meet.

Sociopaths may appear more confident while telling lies than a truth teller does when telling the truth. Why? Perhaps because a truth teller doesn't want to say something inaccurate or dishonest. Because of this, he or she has an internal voice of self-questioning and self-criticism and guards against saying something that might not stand up to the scrutiny, not only of the public, but of conscience. Expert liars, on the other hand, have no such concerns and—once they have made the decision to lie—can speak without internal contradiction. In these cases, the display of absolute confidence betrays the fact something is amiss. In the world of public opinion, though, such confidence is sometimes interpreted as strength, "telling it like it is," directness, and honesty. Novice liars cannot pull this off because they have not fully squashed self-doubt. Once they have crossed the line of expertise, liars can be really dangerous, presenting untruth with a confidence we normally associate with truthfulness. A person's demeanor, even when marked by authenticity, genuineness, and sincerity, does not infallibly indicate honesty.

Only liars' genuine intention to convey fact through their words can do that. And that, to an observer, can be difficult to determine.

Charismatic Totalitarianism: The Political Correlate to Antichrist

Popular depictions of antichrist often portray him as an authoritarian or totalitarian dictator, and we can find some basis for this in Scripture. The book of Revelation, for example, depicts antichrist as holding political power in a charismatic form, as it says he rules by "great wonders," (13:13) deceiving by means of miracles. Revelation also shows his power as authoritarian and dictatorial, indicated by the fact that he compels loyalty by penalty of death, causing "that as many as would not worship the image of the beast should be killed" (v. 15) and forbidding that anyone "might buy or sell, save he that had the mark, or the name of the beast, or the number of his name." (v. 17)

Hannah Arendt (1949/1966), in *The Origins of Totalitarianism*, describes the means by which totalitarian regimes gain control over a population's perceptions of truth by introducing a false narrative that is easier to live with than reality itself:

Before they seize power and establish a world according to their doctrines, totalitarianism movements conjure up a lying world of consistency which is more adequate to the needs of the human mind than reality itself; in which, through sheer imagination, uprooted masses can feel at home and are spared the never-ending shocks which real life and real experiences deal to human beings and their expectations. The force possessed by totalitarian propaganda—before the movements have the power to drop iron curtains to prevent anyone's disturbing, by the slightest reality, the gruesome quiet of an entirely imaginary world—lies in its ability to shut the masses off from the real world. (p. 353)

Our behaviors, more often than we realize, arise from internalized sets of instincts and patterns that inform us how to respond to the situation we find ourselves in. These patterns form in the course of lived experience and come to us through the influence of family and culture. They are also genetically and biologically bestowed on us in ways we do not fully understand. Jungian psychology uses the word *archetype* (Jung, 1948/1969a, p. 133) to describe the most universal and primary patterns, basic forms that seem to underlie our experience of reality. Our behaviors, in this view, rarely arise from scratch. Instead, we rely on unconscious templates to which we hand over control, as though choosing from preprogrammed scripts on a self-driving car. Extreme anxiety can cause us to grab for scripts that, although they quell our immediate sense of alarm, may grossly oversimplify the details of our predicament and leave out information vital to decisions that will serve us in the longer term. Authoritarian rulers excel at activating and amplifying our sense of emergency, increasing their ability to persuade us that we need the certainty they offer. They evoke within us archetypal patterns that hearken to periods when survival depended on unquestioning obedience to a tribe's patriarchal order––a pattern with deep roots in our neurobiology and one we willingly revert to when overwhelmed by confusion, complexity, and ambiguity.

The British psychoanalyst Wilfred Bion (1961/2001) describes our regression to primitive group dynamics as requiring "no training, experience, or mental development. It is instantaneous, inevitable and instinctive." (p. 153) Drawing from his years of experiments in the facilitation of therapeutic groups, Bion observed how groups, at a certain point of anxiety regarding their structure and direction, instinctively select the least qualified member as their leader:

> In its search for a leader the group finds a paranoid schizophrenic or malignant hysteric if possible; failing either of these, a psychopathic personality with delinquent trends will do; failing a psychopathic personality it will pick on the verbally facile high-grade defective. I have at no time experienced a group of more than five people that could not provide a good specimen of one of these.
>
> Once the leader is discovered the group treats him or her with some deference, and the occasional spicing of flattery—"Mr. So-and-so always keeps the discussion going so well"—serves to reinforce his position as leader. (p. 123)

Bion notes that the ineptitude of the leader seems to be the unconscious intention of the selection process and not merely an accidental outcome. He explains that the group seeks someone who can resolve its concerns related to *dependence*, the theme by which it is unconsciously gripped. These concerns include not only the question of whom the group will depend on but also the question of the fate of its most vulnerable member—the one who is most dependent. Bion seems to say that the group, when left to its own devices, selects someone in whom these two poles are evident and who can symbolically resolve the tension between them. Actual leadership ability is of negligible importance in this selection. The leader does more than lead. He or she embodies the paradox necessary for the group's completeness—which emphasizes the leader's essentially charismatic, not managerial, function.

> The belief in the holiness of idiots, the belief that genius is akin to madness, all indicate this same tendency of the group to choose, when left unstructured, its most ill member as its leader. Perhaps it is an unconscious recognition that the baby, if only we had not become accustomed to associating its behaviour with its physical development, is really in-

sane, and . . . it is as necessary to have someone who is dependent as it is to have someone on whom to depend. (p. 122)

Leaders who fulfill our unconscious dependence needs appeal to us on the basis of their charisma rather than on the basis of their administrative competence. Their exercise of authority does not depend on appeal to institutional precedent or norms but on force of personality. They are not bound by ordinary rules or morality because we perceive them as embodying in their essence something more basic to our survival. Laws, ethics, and procedural safeguards pale as mere conventions. We accord unique status to leaders who piggyback upon our instincts for tribal survival, and Freud (1921/1965), in his quasimythical account of society's birth, postulates that their psychology developed along a different course from that of common individuals. "Members of the group were subject to [social] ties just as we see them today, but the father of the primal horde was free. His intellectual acts were strong and independent even in isolation, and his will needed no reinforcement from others." (p. 71) From this, Freud infers:

Consistency leads us to assume that his ego had few libidinal ties; he loved no one but himself, or other people only in so far as they served his needs. To objects his ego gave away no more that was barely necessary.

He, at the very beginning of the history of mankind, was the "superman" whom Nietzsche only expected from the future. Even today the members of a group stand in need of the illusion that they are equally and justly loved by their leader; but the leader himself need love no one else, he may be of a masterful nature, absolutely narcissistic, self-confident and independent. (p. 71)

Scripture echoes psychology's sobering assessment of the character of at least some of the people who readily fill positions of political power. The book of Judges recounts the warning given by Jotham, one of Gilead's sons, to the people of Shechem, after they had selected Abimelech to be their king:

Hearken unto me, ye men of Shechem, that God may hearken unto you.

The trees went forth *on a time* to anoint a king over them; and they said unto the olive tree, Reign thou over us.

But the olive tree said unto them, Should I leave my fatness, wherewith by me they honour God and man, and go to be promoted over the trees?

And the trees said to the fig tree, Come thou, *and* reign over us. But the fig tree said unto them, Should I forsake my sweetness, and my good fruit, and go to be promoted over the trees?

Then said the trees unto the vine, Come thou, *and* reign over us.

And the vine said unto them, Should I leave my wine, which cheereth God and man, and go to be promoted over the trees?

Then said all the trees unto the bramble, Come thou, *and* reign over us.

And the bramble said unto the trees, If in truth ye anoint me king over you, *then* come *and* put your

> trust in my shadow: and if not, let fire
> come out of the bramble, and devour
> the cedars of Lebanon. (Judg. 9:7b–
> 15)

According to Jotham's parable, those who readily accept positions of political power merit suspicion. Their eagerness for power indicates their attempt to fill a personal vacuum, unlike those whose talents and prosocial dispositions allow them to find fulfillment in private life—as the olive tree has its fatness, the fig tree has its sweetness, and the vine has its cheer. Those who perceive political power as a promotion in status are often those who, like the bramble, have qualities that afflict pain, rather than bestow blessings, upon those who take refuge under their cover.

During times of uncertainty, we are at risk of submitting ourselves, not just to leaders who do not have our interests in mind, but to unconscious templates for survival that do not adequately account for factors civilization relies upon. We may have to live with the consequences of these choices long after the period of their apparent usefulness. Authoritarian leaders can temporarily alleviate the anxiety of participation in a complex and diverse society. We exchange the exertion of understanding and intention required for observance of society's rule of law for an unconscious fantasy of dependence upon an all-sustaining guide and provider. Societal structures, which depend on our consensus for their existence, crumble in the process.

III.

ANTICHRIST IN
CONTEXT OF
PSYCHE AND SACRED

III.

Antichrist in Context of Psyche and Sacred

Antichrist as Archetypal Shadow

The observation that antichrist falls radically outside the range of our normal expectations is consistent with the understanding of antichrist as an expression of an *archetypal shadow.* Carl Jung used the term *shadow* (Jung, 1948/1969b, p. 8) to designate characteristics we possess that remain outside our awareness because they go against our conscious understanding, the story we tell ourselves about who we are. In our own imaginations, we see ourselves as one kind of person. We often fail to recognize those aspects of ourselves that do not fit into that image. We may readily see those qualities in others and feel either positively or negatively toward those people to the same degree with which we remain unconscious of those qualities in ourselves. Shadows exist for each of us as individuals and for entire cultures, which have their own biases, sets of values, and notions of progress, and consciously and unconsciously marginalize and repress expressions that do not accord with those ideals.

In addition to individual and cultural shadows, Jung (1948/1969b) hypothesized that shadows can exist on a yet-deeper layer of existence—the *archetypal* (p. 10)—in which the repressed material is scandalous to the self-understanding not merely of an individual or a culture but to the configuration of reality itself. While it may be difficult for us to conceptualize the idea of an archetypal shadow, perhaps we can find an analogy in astrophysics' *dark matter* and *dark energy*—which, although they make up 95% of the universe, are beyond our ability to measure with any of our existing scientific instruments. NASA (n.d.) notes the remarkable nature of this fact:

> More is unknown than is known. We know how much dark energy there is because we know how it affects the universe's expansion. Other than that, it is a complete mystery. But it is an

important mystery. It turns out that roughly 68% of the universe is dark energy. Dark matter makes up about 27%. The rest—everything on Earth, everything ever observed with all of our instruments, all normal matter—adds up to less than 5% of the universe. Come to think of it, maybe it shouldn't be called "normal" matter at all, since it is such a small fraction of the universe.

When shadows assert themselves (as they inevitably do, because they are part of reality, though we have not recognized them as such), we experience them as disruptive to our customary understanding—seeming to come from an alien source. They appear as improbable, and perhaps even impossible, given our ordinary frame of reference. Archetypal shadows, in particular, can appear as intrusions from another realm, something supernatural—perhaps angelic or demonic, depending on whether they signify something hopeful or foreboding. They appear as something uncanny and spooky, not merely an extension of reality as we know it. They exist so far from the statistical mean that they seem, as much as anything possibly can, to come out of nowhere. Such events, when they occur in the field of economics, have been labeled *black swans*. In the field of nonlinear optics, they are represented by the phenomenon of the *rogue wave*—a term that has also come to describe massive, seemingly unpredictable waves as they appear in the ocean (Dudley et al., 2020).

Considered as a shadow, antichrist brings to our attention aspects of ourselves and reality that we habitually suppress and repress. In its capacity as shadow, when antichrist appears, it represents what Freud (1915/1953) described as the "return of the repressed" (p. 93)—something we have pushed aside and stuffed down that we simply cannot hold down any longer, which erupts into awareness in a surprising and sometimes catastrophic way. Jung (1959/1969) considered antichrist a manifestation of a deep psychological counterbalance necessary to correct a one-sided construct of goodness that emerged as a result of the Christian revelation (pp. 36-71). He believed that Christianity, with its emphasis on light and spirit, set up a situation in which some important aspects of life and nature were expelled from our personal and cultural awareness. When we experience them, we attempt to deny them as genuine aspects of our own identities. Antichrist appears when these aspects of life and nature can no longer bear repression—when we must encounter, in a decisive way, the side of reality we have steadfastly kept out of view. The appearance of antichrist is thus a cataclysmic corrective to our one-sided understanding of who and what we are, and our understanding of reality itself. Seen in this way, the appearance of antichrist is possibly an avoidable event—if we can listen and proactively respond to indications of what our cultural one-sidedness has repressed. (I explore this possibility in my doctoral dissertation, Skidmore, R., 2017, *Inanna and the Lion: Patriarchy Transformed Through Listening to the Suffering Feminine*.)

Considered on the archetypal level, antichrist appears not as a mere extension of our normal perceptions and projections of reality but as a determinant of them. It appears as something that assertively shapes our experience of reality, rather than fitting into our customary concepts and experiences. Of the various ways of looking at antichrist discussed so far, this archetypal perspective most closely matches the idea of antichrist that commonly emerges from the interpretation of Scripture. From this archetypal perspective, the power antichrist exerts over the world and surrounding reality is not explainable merely by understanding the intrapsychic psychological dynamics of the person who is antichrist—whether those dynamics include narcissism, sociopathy, or not. Nor is it explainable merely by understanding the meaning that a significant portion of the population projects upon him (or her, or them). While the explanation for his influence as an archetype includes both these intrapsychic and sociological elements, it ultimately transcends them.

According to this archetypal perspective, and according to the perspective commonly attributed to Scripture, antichrist's appearance brings with it a change in the configuration of reality itself—so that, in addition to necessary psychological and social factors coming into play, corresponding political and economic events fall into place as if on cue, and even events in the natural world and on the scale of astronomy seem to bear witness to the way history has mysteriously altered its course. It is as though a new or previously unseen riverbed appears—"the river of Antichrist," we might call it—and everything that makes up our personal, social, and cosmic reality begins to flow along its course with apparently unstoppable momentum. Or, it is as though we have entered an astrological constellation in which everything is spiritually determined by this theme.

Antichrist as Expression of Evil

As we approach the realization of antichrist as an expression of archetypal shadow, we feel increasingly tempted to apply the word *evil* to designate what we encounter. *Evil* is perhaps the word best suited to describe our encounters with malevolent forces that seem to originate from a preternatural source. In this way, evil presents as something maliciously and radically disruptive to the cosmic, moral, and social order we depend upon for our existence. As an archetypal construct, it defies our attempts to understand it merely as an expression of our own personal or collective moral failings. Instead, evil presents itself as an autonomous entity with its own principle of life, consciousness, and determination.

This question, though—of whether evil is an aspect of ourselves or if it comes from radically beyond us—has immense psychological and spiritual importance. At the point we conclude that evil comes from a source completely outside ourselves, we forfeit our opportunity to receive and integrate information it might bring to us about our own blind spots and about how we can understand ourselves in more adequate ways. We also put evil beyond the reach of our powers of reason, where we have hope, if there is any, of understanding its origins and how we might avoid it. This might explain our historical reluctance to resort to radical explanations for the origin of evil. Arendt (1949/1966) says:

> It is inherent in our entire philosophical tradition that we cannot conceive of a "radical evil," and this is true both for Christian theology, which conceded even to the Devil himself a celestial origin, as well as for Kant, the only philosopher who, in the word he coined for it, at least must have suspected the existence of this evil even though he immediately rationalized it in the concept of a "perverted ill will" that could be explained by comprehensible motives. (p. 459)

Arendt acknowledges, though, how our insistence on rational explanations for evil leave us partially unsatisfied. "Therefore, we actually have nothing to fall back on in order to understand a phenomenon that nevertheless confronts us with its overpowering reality and breaks down all standards we know," (p. 459) she says. Explanations of evil as radical, though, can also cause us to lose sight of the underlying humanity of people we label in this way—putting them outside the range of our possible understanding and compassion. For this reason, although radical evil exists as a conceptual possibility, we have reason to exercise caution in applying it to actual persons—perhaps especially when our application of the label antichrist might have already inclined us toward overlooking the humanity of those we ascribe it to.

Differences Between Religious and Psychological Understandings of Antichrist

As noted, the understanding of antichrist as an archetypal shadow most closely resembles the common religious understanding of antichrist. However, the psychological understanding includes aspects the religious perspective does not usually emphasize. The psychological understanding of shadow—whether on a personal or archetypal level—includes the ideal of integration, meaning that the qualities of the shadow are recognized as disowned parts of the self and that we ultimately benefit from an expanded self-understanding in which we give them some place. Integration may result in us seeing ourselves in less idealized ways.

We may lose the satisfaction of believing we are always good or right. We may lose the certainty with which we judge others as wrong or evil. What we gain, however, is a greater sense of wholeness, flexibility, and affinity with others and the surrounding world. We experience a relaxation of the ceaseless war with all that we once so adamantly opposed, now viewing the struggle as one of creative interaction, engagement, and potential improvement, rather than one in which annihilation of what we oppose is the primary aim.

In the case of an archetypal shadow in which the cosmos itself seems to be in the grip of a power that turns individuals, society, and even nature itself into enemies of good, the psychological perspective would go so far as to suggest that even a radically dire situation is still but part of a process toward greater balance and, that once we've received the shadow's shock and scandal, we can get on with a more realistic understanding of ourselves and reality. This perspective admittedly presents problems, though. Are there not evils we must resist in an unqualified manner and not merely as part of a process of integration? Religious and moral perspectives often stress the need to oppose evil without compromise—and, in the process, take it for granted that evil can be definitively identified.

In reality, though, the depth psychological and religious perspectives are not necessarily mutually exclusive, and they can complement each other. The religious perspective, even when it purports to identify unambiguous instances of evil, carefully acknowledges that the moral clarity necessary for such absolute judgments resides in God alone—and that we, in ourselves, do not so wholly identify with the good that we can oppose evil from the standpoint of our own egoic perspective. The epistle of Jude offers this cryptic allusion: "Yet Michael the archangel, when contending with the devil he disputed about the body of Moses, durst not bring against him a railing accusation, but said, The Lord rebuke thee" (1:9); and the book of Acts offers the cautionary tale of the seven sons of Sceva, who tried to cast out a demon by their own authority: "And the evil spirit answered and said, Jesus I know, and Paul I know; but who are ye? And the man in whom the evil spirit was leaped on them, and overcame them, and prevailed against them, so that they fled out of that house naked and wounded." (Ac. 19:15–16) In other words, from the religious perspective, we are summoned to resist evil but not to forget, in the process, that we are not God. Further, the religious perspective does indeed contain its own vision of ultimate integration, in which, "when all things shall be subdued unto him, then shall the Son also himself be subject unto him that put all things under him, that God may be all in all." (1 Co. 15:28) Christian history includes voices that express hope even for the salvation of demons themselves. St Isaac of Syria (trans. 1989), in the seventh century C.E. described the "compassionate heart" as one that is "on fire for the whole of creation, for humanity, for the birds, for the animals, for demons and all that exists." (p. 29)

Conversely, the integrative vision of the depth psychological perspective is not one that necessarily can, or should, be exhaustively realized within the life of a single person. A person who attempts to embrace within her or himself all possibility, by never choosing any one thing in a decisive way, avoids the element of sacrifice necessary for the development of an ego that acknowledges its own finite nature as well as the formation of a moral perspective in which terms such as courage, hope, and integrity retain their usual meanings. The religious perspective often emphasizes this need to choose.

Finally, the task of integrating disowned aspects of our identity and the task of addressing and confronting problematic elements in the external environment or in the behaviors of others often go hand in hand. They are not mutually exclusive. The question, "Does this fault exist in the other, or in myself?" often yields a both-and, rather than an either-or answer. To recognize that I harbor the racism I see in someone else, for example, does not require that I consider my perception of it in the other as only an illusion. Having addressed racism in myself, the behavior that requires addressing may still remain in the other or in the external environment. I can make this assessment more clearly, though, and act without impulsivity, if I first tend to the part in myself that suffers from it. "First cast out the beam out of thine own eye; and then shalt thou see clearly to cast out the mote out of thy brother's eye," (Mt. 7:5) Christ says. In general, if we focus entirely on our own internal qualities, or focus entirely on those qualities as they exist outside of us, we miss some of the opportunity for growth and change to which our awareness invites us.

IV.

ANTICHRIST'S SOCIAL DYNAMICS

IV.

Antichrist's Social Dynamics

Antichrist as Expressive of Group Dynamics

Reflection upon the identity and psychological constitution of antichrist often focuses exclusively on the collection of personal traits that comprise him (or her, or them). This approach underemphasizes ways in which antichrist's identity might be a manifestation of public projection. Similar to other social roles—that of the *scapegoat*, for example—antichrist potentially acquires his significance from the meanings others bestow upon him through their projection of group needs and functions. Social groups maintain their homeostasis through conscious and unconscious assignment of roles and tasks. Members of a group finding themselves suddenly stranded in a hostile desert, for example, may spontaneously generate a structure that includes a leader, someone who keeps a record of conversations, someone who proposes bold actions, and someone who serves as a voice of caution. The group will also assign various material tasks to particular individuals, such as guarding the camp or going out to hunt for resources. From this initial configuration, there might also emerge someone who pacifies animosities as they appear, someone who voices encouragement when the group feels disheartened, and a vulnerable one, whom the group deems as the one especially in need of protection. In times of stress, it would not be surprising if an individual, or some subset of the group, became the target of blame—the scapegoat.

While each of these group roles indicates something about the characteristics of each person who fills them, they say just as much about the psychological needs of the other members of the group and of the group as a whole. The difference between a role and an identity is that a role, if one person leaves it vacant, is usually filled by another, because the group structure itself requires that someone occupy that position (Agazarian & Peters, 1981, p. 104). Viewing antichrist in this way, we would not expect to grasp the meaning of antichrist simply by looking at the individual who fills that role. A full understanding would require understanding the motivations of the entire group, of which antichrist is an expression. They, after all, are the ones who conspire, consciously and unconsciously, to prop up this particular person in that role.

Antichrist as a Label Versus Antichrist as an Operative Principle

An important question arises from this consideration of antichrist as a social role. How do we identify who fulfills this position for a particular group? To answer this, we need to differentiate between the process in which a group labels someone as antichrist—and the person or thing that actually functions for the group in that role. These are distinct from each other yet relate to each other in important ways.

Antichrist as a Label

Christian sects have often tried to identify individuals to whom they might apply the label antichrist. Hal Lindsey's 1970 *The Late, Great Planet Earth* purported to provide a road map for Christian evangelicals hungry for information about the end times, including how they might recognize the Antichrist. More recently, Tim LaHaye and Jerry Jenkins cast end-times events in their *Left Behind* novel series—with, again, Antichrist as a central figure. It is a common trope among some Protestant Christians to identify antichrist with popes of the Roman Catholic Church. More recently still, some Christian groups identified Barack Obama as the Antichrist.

This labeling process reveals important things. First, a group's understanding of antichrist—specifically, whom and what they label as anti-christ—can reveal much about what group members mean when they say they believe in Christ. It is common knowledge that a variety of expressions of Christianity exists and that the differences among them include more than just differences in style of worship. Each Christian group, community, or denomination has its own way of understanding what it means to be a Christian in the world, and these differences in understanding manifest in an ethos, an aesthetic, and in social and political involvement of one kind or another. It is sometimes difficult to classify these distinguishing characteristics. It can help to pay attention not only to what a group or individuals say they believe about Christ but to observe whom and what they consider to be antichrist. Just as we understand north in relation to south, so we may not be able adequately to understand a community's conception of Christ unless we know how that community conceives of antichrist. This may help us make sense of the sometimes extreme differences in the way different Christian groups express and promote their values and cultures.

Antichrist as an Operative Principle

The recognition of unconscious psychological dynamics—which apply as much to group as to individual psychology—raises the possibility that what a group consciously considers to be antichrist may not be identical to what, in fact, functions as antichrist for them. The former, their conscious articulation of who or what antichrist is, may often express the group's shadow and indicate its scapegoat more than it reflects awareness of who or what actually has the potential to steal the group's allegiance away from Christ.

Recognizing this functional aspect of the notion of antichrist brings us to consider, again, the relationship between antichrist and idolatry. Scripturally and theologically, one's embrace of an idol renders it impossible for her or him—or for a group—to simultaneously accord to God the worship appropriate to God, in God's capacity as that which alone is worthy of utmost adoration. We can imagine various ways an idol might do this, in addition to perhaps the most obvious way, in which it becomes an outright substitute and replacement for God in the human heart or in group consciousness. These other ways might include the idol's ability to effectively distract worshippers so that they cannot adequately consolidate their attention upon God, and its ability to distort worship so that, while what they worship still bears the name of *God*, it no longer reflects the transcendence or character that Scripture or theology historically attributes to God—nor does it represent an object that elicits maximal aspiration on the part of the human psyche. It depletes the name *God* of meaning, by applying it to something ultimately less than or other than God.

V.

ASSESSMENT OF A DANGEROUS IDEA

V.

Assessment of a Dangerous Idea

Usefulness of the Antichrist Concept

This writing promised to address the question of whether antichrist terminology has value for us today. Though the answer to that is not unequivocal, I suggest yes. For one, antichrist's persistence as a religious, social, and psychological construct indicates its archetypal nature. Archetypes do not go away just because we are oblivious to them or actively ignore them. Archetypes (though our understanding of them continues to evolve) spell out the contours of patterns deeply present in reality—and we encounter these patterns, even if we lack the mental conceptions that, when they function optimally, help us navigate the terrain these patterns compose. When deprived of our conscious consideration, they exercise their influence upon us unconsciously, in their most basic and primitive forms. Our failure to subject the notion of antichrist to thoughtful analysis—perhaps because we consider it too religious, primitive, or archaic to warrant serious attention—increases, not decreases, the likelihood that it will catch hold of the reins of our perceptions and lead us toward attitudes and actions that subvert our best judgments of reason and morality. The label "antichrist," for better or worse, designates a part of the map of reality we have inherited. It can serve us to revise and refine this part of the map. Simply expunging it, on the other hand, destines us to travel without awareness over its territory, unprepared for what it presents.

The usefulness of the concept of antichrist depends on whether it highlights information that alerts us to things important to our well-being. I believe it can do this in several ways. For one, it can bring awareness to religious communities of their own shadows. Antichrist personifies and potentially embodies the possibility of betraying Christ in the name of Christ. Acknowledging that such a possibility exists—that is, to acknowledge the reality of antichrist—means admitting the possibility of radical self-deception and the capacity of religious values to become inverted. This admission, though, requires moral and epistemic humility, without which the risk of religion inflicting harm increases.

The concept of antichrist, in addition to representing the epitome of extreme danger in spiritual life, can serve as a useful analogue to extreme dangers as they appear in the social, psychological, and political realms. The explanation for extreme-case scenarios lies outside our ordinary frames of reference and requires language that conveys the transcendence and autonomy with which such phenomena confront us. It was this that led Le Bon (1896/2001), in his 1896 study, *The Crowd*, to resort to religious language to describe the nature of thought, feeling, and behavior that appears in public gatherings.

> When these convictions are closely examined, whether at epochs marked by fervent religious faith, or by great political upheavals such as those of the last century, it is apparent that they always assume a peculiar form which I cannot better define than by giving it the name of a religious senti-ment. (p. 43)

The use of religious language is appropriate because, at the point where conventional language falters, the characteristics being described are increasingly indistinguishable from those that are distinctly religious. Le Bon continues:

> A person is not religious solely when he worships a divinity, but when he puts all the resources of his mind, the complete submission of his will, and the whole-souled ardour of fanaticism at the service of a cause or an individual who becomes the goal and guide of his thoughts and actions. (p. 43)

Finally, antichrist terminology is indispensable in some situations because alternate terms, from nonreligious frames of reference, do not adequately describe the dynamics that are being discussed. For example, if a political figure assumes a place of honor that supplants the worship of Christ in a Christian community or individual, describing that person as incompetent, corrupt, or malevolent—while this may be accurate—fails to describe what makes his (or her, or their) role uniquely pernicious to the spiritual health of that community or individual. The term "antichrist" has no rival in referring to that, specifically. Likewise, descriptions of incompetence, corruption, and malevolence do not in themselves account for the constellation of factors that indicate the appearance of antichrist—which, as an archetypal formation, is greater than the sum of these parts.

From a religious standpoint, the concept of antichrist represents the ultimate risk to our ability to retain our connection to truth—and the ultimate attack upon truth itself. Eliminating the idea of antichrist, because it seems antiquated or obsolete, invites the question of what more adequate concept can fill that role. For Christian communities, antichrist likely continues to be the most acute expression of our vulnerability to deception and, especially, self-deception. For the concept of antichrist to function for us in this way, we need to rethink it—to deliver it from its most common use: our musing about how contemporary events might reflect the literal fulfillment of biblical prophecy. Instead, we need to emphasize antichrist as a spirit that can appear in multiple individuals and situations, and especially how it can appear within the biases and assumptions of our own spiritual perspective—appearing as "an angel of light" (2. Cor. 11:14) in every instance. For antichrist to function as a useful concept, we must move beyond our understanding of it merely as a label and instead view it as the designation of an autonomous and transcendent archetypal reality around which our understanding can continue to deepen as we reflect upon it.

Caution in Use of Antichrist Terminology

Antichrist's usefulness as a concept also depends on awareness of the potential perils in its use. When we use it to identify who or what functions as antichrist for someone else, if we have a mature perspective, we will first scrutinize ourselves for ways in which our judgments might be projections of our own lapses and failures. Doing this entails awareness of the possibility that our conscious perspective includes elements of self-deception or ignorance. Individuals or communities with a religious orientation can find this especially challenging because they frequently identify their religious perspective with what is unequivocally good, but a mature perspective understands that the thing it labels as antichrist in the other may be present to some degree in oneself. This does not mean that antichrist never has a legitimate external reference—but that mature use of the label requires not exempting oneself from the same judgment.

Engaging in intensive psychoanalysis—and confession, its spiritual counterpart—can contribute to the self-awareness that can moderate the risks of projection.

Those with a mature perspective will apply special caution when using the term antichrist to denote a particular, contemporary individual as the fulfillment of biblical prophecies concerning the antichrist. Using it this way amounts to the declaration of an imminent spiritual threat, of global and historic significance. The claim that this or that person is the antichrist, without explanation of the spiritual, psychological, and social context in which it is made, fails to provide its hearers with the information necessary for useful response. It announces the apocalypse as a sheer and present fact yet fails to account for ways such an announcement likely strengthens the very polarities and unconscious projections that contributed to the emergence of apocalyptic dynamics in the first place. It fails to illuminate the role our own spiritual condition has in the appearance of these apocalyptic events and the way, through vigilance, self-critique, and integration, we might reestablish conditions of wholeness, morality, and justice. For Christian communities, this means restored allegiance to Christ as the revelation of God,

Himself, not merely in verbal attestation (which is rarely formally compromised in Christian communities, anyway, even when their use of the name Christ has lost connection with its transcendent point of reference) but as their actual operational principle.

Conclusion

My introduction intimated that I see a connection between these reflections upon antichrist and our current political reality, predominated by Donald Trump. I acknowledge that I cannot make such an application without crossing an existential divide, across which I cannot compel a reader to go except through suggestion. To those who do not cross, I will seem to have gone too far—perhaps even into territory where I deserve to be dismissed or ridiculed. In response to such potential critics, I remind them that not to cross entails just as much choice and responsibility as to cross.

If we steer away from the idea that Trump evokes antichrist themes, here too we venture an existential claim—one that implies the notion of antichrist, which serves to alert us to spiritual danger, registers no danger when it looks to Trump. To this I answer, "If not here, where?" and, "If not now, when?" This claim, which is no more immune from scrutiny than my own, requires a corresponding understanding of reality in which Trump does not present a critical affront to essential elements of moral and spiritual well-being and that a person who believes otherwise misunderstands him. People can hold this perspective if their notions of Christ, on the one hand, and Donald Trump, on the other, do not decisively collide. I contend that avoiding such a collision requires distortion and error, either in the exercise of spiritual and moral discernment, or in the appraisal of facts. Further, I dare to believe the latter can be rectified, if the one in error possesses the will.

My application of thoughts about antichrist to Donald Trump entails a straddling of spiritual and political perspectives that some will perhaps not consider appropriate. I accept this as yet another risk of my approach because I believe to refrain from it invites the yet-greater risk of disengaging politics from our capacity for theological, moral, and spiritual discernment—and, conversely, rendering theological and spiritual discernment powerless to address political realities, however much they are part and parcel of human society. The cost on both sides, I believe, is too high.

The alarm I am convinced needs to be sounded about Donald Trump concerns the threat he poses to our deep moral and spiritual faculties, from which issue not just our electoral decisions but our valuation of civilization and culture per se. Ultimately, the alarm signals a crisis that threatens our image of humanity—threatens to destroy hope that we, as human beings, can be motivated by more than craven self-interest, hatred, fear, and greed. This severing of the thread of hope in humanity's positive potential affronts not merely the humanistic ideals of the Enlightenment—though it does do that. It also poses a direct challenge to one of the sources of inspiration for those ideals: the theological understanding of humanity as made in the image of God, summoned to a potential that bespeaks its divine origin and purpose. The scriptural description of this threat, in the theological realm, resides in St. John's first epistle:

> Every spirit that confesseth that Jesus
> Christ is come in the flesh is of God:
> And every spirit that confesseth not
> that Jesus Christ is come in the flesh
> is not of God: and this is that *spirit* of
> antichrist, whereof ye have heard that
> it should come; and even now already
> is it in the world. (1 Jn. 4:2–3)

It takes little imagination to transpose this theological threat to the social, psychological, and political realm.

Some moments in history cannot be compartmentalized as having only relative importance because they impinge upon matters fundamental to our apprehension of truth. The philosopher Gabriel Marcel (1973) argued this of the situation presented by Hitler prior to his invasion of Czechoslovakia—a threat the Allies failed to respond to, when it could have made a difference.

> In what conditions, then, can we establish a connection between occasion and truth, such that to miss the occasion would amount to being on the side of error? I would say that in this perspective the case of Hitlerism appears privileged in a certain way. For Hitler's enterprise was directed against what could be called human order, or the human community considered in its universality. Consequently the occasion, the *kairos*, here takes on a positive value, since it designates the possibility of stopping

short an enterprise founded on
contempt for all right. (p. 97)

Antichrist terminology, used cautiously, may play a
role in describing these situations—occasionally
encountered in the midst of politics as usual—in
which our response may determine matters of
fundamental moral and spiritual importance.

In those rare cases when a mature spiritual
perspective dares to suggest that the spirit of
antichrist appears to be constellating and localizing
in the actions and character of a specific individual,
it will acknowledge that the actual identity of
antichrist lies beyond what we can conclusively
know from our finite frame of reference—that we
have the ability only to note how a particular
individual appears, increasingly, to embody the
themes and functions scripturally, socially, and
psychologically associated with antichrist. And one
can go no further than this in describing Donald
Trump.

References

Agazarian, Y., & Peters, R. (1981). *The visible and invisible group: Two perspectives on group psychotherapy and group process.* Karnac.

American Psychiatric Association. (2013). *Diagnostic and statistical manual of mental disorders* (5th ed.).

Arendt, H. (1966). *The origins of totalitarianism.* Harcourt, Brace, and World, Inc. (Original work published 1949)

Bion, W. (2001). *Experiences in groups, and other papers.* Routledge. (Original work published 1961)

Dudley, J. M., Dias, F., Erkintalo, M., & Genty, G. (2013). *Instabilities, breathers and rogue*

waves in optics. https://arxiv.org/pdf/
1410.3071.pdf.

Freud, S. (1965). *Group psychology and the analysis of the ego* (J. Strachey, Trans.). Bantam. (Original work published 1921)

Freud, S. (1953). Repression. In E. Jones (Ed.), *Sigmund Freud, M.D., L.L.D.: Collected papers* (Vol. 4, pp. 84-97). The Hogarth Press. https://archive.org/details/in.ernet. dli.2015.52969/page/n97/mode/2up. (Original work published 1915)

Jung, C. (1969a). Instinct and the unconscious (R. F. C. Hull, Trans.). In H. Read, M. Fordham, G. Adler, & W. McGuire (Eds.), *The collected works of C. G. Jung* (2nd ed., Vol. 8, pp. 129-138). Princeton University Press. (Original work published 1948)

Jung, C. (1969b). The shadow (R. F. C. Hull, Trans.). In H. Read, M. Fordham, G. Adler, & W. McGuire (Eds.), *The collected works of C. G. Jung* (2nd ed., Vol. 9, Pt. 2, pp. 8-10). Princeton University Press. (Original work published 1948)

Jung, C. (1969). Christ, a symbol of the self: Researches into the phenomenology of the self (R. F. C. Hull, Trans.). In H. Read, M. Fordham, G. Adler, & W. McGuire (Eds.), *The collected works of C. G. Jung* (2nd ed., Vol. 9, Pt. 2, pp. 36-71). Princeton University Press. (Original work published 1959)

Le Bon, G. (2001). *The crowd: A study of the popular mind*. Kitchener, Batoche, 2001. (Original work published 1896)

Marcel, G. (1973). Truth and concrete situations. In *Tragic wisdom and beyond: Including conversations between Paul Ricoeur and Gabriel Marcel* (pp. 91-103) (S. Jolin & P. McCormick, Trans.). Northwestern University.

NASA, Dark Energy, Dark Matter (n.d.). *Science Mission Directorate | Science*. https://science. nasa.gov/astrophysics/focus-areas/what-is-dark-energy.

Skidmore, R. C. (2017). *Inanna and the lion: Patriarchy transformed through listening to the suffering feminine* (Order No. 10639004)

[Doctoral dissertation, Pacifica Graduate Institute]. ProQuest Central. (1968593394).

St. Isaac of Syria. (1989). *Daily readings with St. Isaac of Syria* (S. Brock, Trans.) (A. M. Allchin, Ed.). Springfield, IL: Templegate.

CPSIA information can be obtained
at www.ICGtesting.com
Printed in the USA
FSHW011722151020
74775FS

9 781630 518950